Furry Logic

DON'T WORRY!

For Clare and Jamie

Jane Seabrook & Ashleigh Brilliant

Furry Logic

DON'T WORRY!

Ten Speed Press

Berkeley

Please remain calm,

until the situation gets completely

out of control.

Don't be afraid—

I'm right behind you,

using you as a shield.

We must move with

the times, as soon as

the times are sure which

way they're moving.

The good news is that

the bad news is not much worse

than usual.

Some days are better than others.

This, unfortunately,

is one of the others.

Facts should never be faced

too early in the morning.

Once I get started,

nothing can stop me,

but sometimes it seems that

nothing can start me.

At my current rate of progress,

I'll soon be somewhere behind

my starting point.

Things are gradually falling into place

on top of me.

I could try resigning myself

to fate—

but what if fate refuses to accept

my resignation?

Reality is starin

who will be th

...e in the face—

...rst to blink?

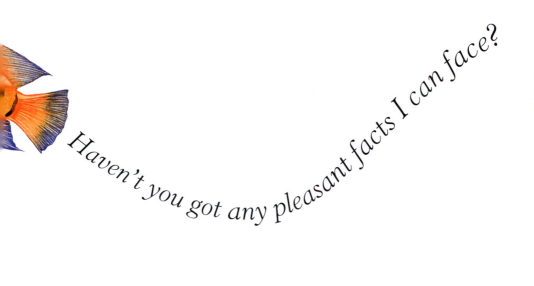

Haven't you got any pleasant facts I can face?

Why is everybody behaving

as if there were

no reason

o panic?

Try to relax

and enjoy the crisis.

Don't rush me—

I'll make the wrong decision

when I'm good and ready.

Don't let success go to your head—

and, if you fail,

don't let failure go there either.

I can't believe that from so little,

I've made so little.

Be thankful for what we have,

even if it's only

each other.

If you take care   of yourself, that will t

...ne less person you have to worry about.

One of my clever ways

of fighting back against the world

is by boldly going to bed.

Please excuse my occasional smiles—I'

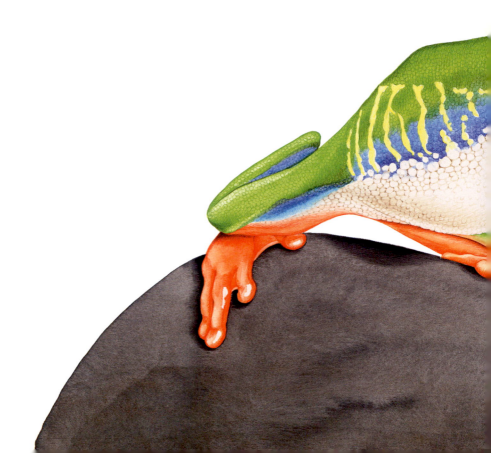

ill recovering from an attack of optimism.

I keep having a strange,

uneasy premonition

that everything is going

to be all right.

urprises me by working exactly

as it should.

There's a better time

coming—its name is

lunch.

Life is short: have another

piece of   chocolate.

Do something

mportant with your life: enjoy it!

Artist's Notes

I'm a natural-born worrier, endowed from birth with that nagging little "worry" gene. But a television documentary I watched recently has given me a different perspective on my worries.

Life After People is a documentary that deals with what would happen if humans vanished from the earth. A depressing thought at first glance, but perhaps there's more to the story. Nature is so powerful and so relentless that about a hundred years after people vanished from the planet, she would have corroded, eroded, and demolished, in one way or another, all of our man-made structures and environmental catastrophes to cover the planet in greenery and wildlife once again.

So how does that help me to get my worries in perspective?

1. Nature will clean up all our messes eventually; everything will be fixed, everything will eventually be OK.
2. Whatever happens, we are but a tiny blip. Therefore, we might as well stop worrying about the small stuff, because in the Grand Scheme of Things, even the things we think are really big are actually tiny.
3. If there is no point in worrying . . . then we may as well be happy. It is as simple and as difficult as that.

If we can aim to be more happy, more of the time, then we are winning. I hope you have enjoyed this book and that it has given you a small respite from some of your worries. I always enjoy receiving your comments and suggestions via my website, www.furrylogicbooks.com.

Best wishes,

Jane.

Furry Logic Who's Who

This page is one of the most fun to compile. It's where all these eclectic creatures get to be together in a few colorful pages, from the less familiar korhaan to one of my favorite painting subjects, the blue and yellow macaw. In order of appearance they are:

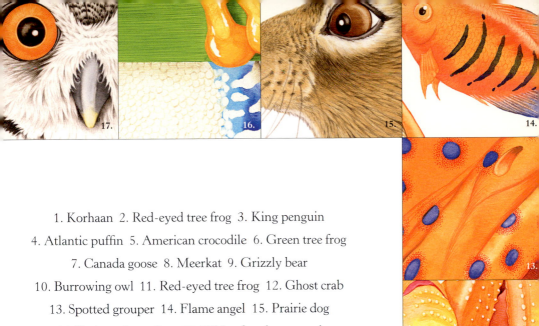

1. Korhaan 2. Red-eyed tree frog 3. King penguin
4. Atlantic puffin 5. American crocodile 6. Green tree frog
7. Canada goose 8. Meerkat 9. Grizzly bear
10. Burrowing owl 11. Red-eyed tree frog 12. Ghost crab
13. Spotted grouper 14. Flame angel 15. Prairie dog
16. Red-eyed tree frog 17. White-faced scops owl
18. Blue-footed booby 19. Ostrich
20. Grevy's zebra

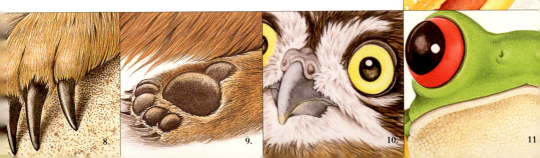

Furry Logic Who's Who

21. Tabby cat 22. Harvest mouse 23. Red-eyed tree frog
24. Grizzly bear 25. Chameleon 26. Lunch
27. Blue and yellow macaw 28. Lunch 29. Chipmunk
30. Gentoo penguin 31. Ladybug

Jane Seabrook is an illustrator and designer who works from home in her country studio on the outskirts of Auckland, New Zealand. She shares her life with her husband, two adult children, and three utterly adorable Birman cats.
For more information, including how to purchase any of the original paintings that appear in this book,
visit www.furrylogicbooks.com.

Other Books by Jane Seabrook

Furry Logic: A Guide to Life's Little Challenges

Furry Logic Parenthood

Furry Logic Laugh at Life

The Pick of Furry Logic

Furry Logic Wild Wisdom

Purry Logic

28.   29.   30.   31.

Thank you!

Acknowledgments

I would like to say a big thank-you to Ashleigh Brilliant, whose Pot-Shot series of epigrams provided the words for this book. There are approximately 10,000 epigrams in Ashleigh's Pot-Shot collection, so for an artist like me, searching for the right words to go with my paintings, it is the perfect treasure trove of inspiration.

For thousands more Ashleigh Brilliant Pot-Shots or for more information about his work, visit www.ashleighbrilliant.com.

Thank you to everyone at Ten Speed Press for all their support and encouragement, especially my editor, Lisa Westmoreland.

Thank you also to Alex Trimbach and Troy Caltaux at Image Centre in Auckland, New Zealand, and to Debby Heard Photography.

Library of Congress Cataloging-in-Publication Data
Seabrook, Jane.
Furry logic : don't worry! / by Jane Seabrook.
    p. cm.
Summary: "A new collection of watercolor animals and inspirational sayings,
featuring critters who get tough—and get going—in the face of troubled times"
—Provided by publisher.
  1. Conduct of life—Humor. 2. Animals—Pictorial works. I. Title.
PN6231.C6142S427 2009
818'.602—dc22
                                         2009010356

ISBN 978-1-58008-819-0

Printed in China

10 9 8 7 6 5 4 3 2 1

First Edition